HOW TO MEDITATE?

How I stopped doubting meditation, applied simple steps and discovered a 10 minute routine to a successful life

Olivia Smith

Contents

Introduction

Are you stressed at work or in life? Do you feel that you are lacking productivity or feeling depressed? Are you looking for a way to cope with the daily stress or depression? Did you know that even kids can practice meditation to cope with their anxiety problems? Do you know that meditation will not only help deal with stress but also helps you to lead a successful life? If you feel you can relate to any of these or if you would like to start including meditation or mindfulness as one of your daily exercise routines feel free to go ahead and read the rest of this book. This book provides a practical and no fuss way for starting meditation or mindfulness.

In today's fast moving and busy world, learning to meditate can bring a sense of calm and inner satisfaction. The practice of meditation is a gateway into your mind and into your inner consciousness. This results in an enhanced awareness of your own existence and your overall relationship to the cosmos.

You might have an age-old question, "Who am I and why am I here?" or you may be looking to implement simple relaxation techniques. Meditation may just be the answer for you so why not give it a try.

How to meditate is really up to the individual. There are hundreds of meditation techniques. You can pick and choose from different schools of thought and find a way of doing things that best suits your personality. However, although deep thinking has many different cultural contexts, there are certain general parts which go beyond the bounds of any one clearly particular culture.

According to Eastern beliefs, to meditate means to think on the eternal, or rather to expand your awareness until you are at one with cosmos as a whole. Feelings like sadness, joy or even love can fade away, but the universe is forever. Eventually, with practice, learning to meditate can bring you in closer attunement with the very root and purpose of existence itself.

Even if you are not interested in the transcendental implications of meditation, meditating will provide undeniable health benefits. Meditation can have positive effects on stress induced illness such as heart disease and high blood pressure. In conjunction with traditional Western approaches to medicine, meditation can target the root causes behind stress-based conditions by calming and clearing the mind.

Many relaxation techniques include meditation. You can meditate sitting in the chair or on the floor, standing or lying down. It is not difficult to learn how to meditate. There are many online programs that can teach you the basics and help you get started. These programs can guide you every step of the process of meditation, give you tips on the appropriate posture and teach you how to create the ideal setting for your meditation session.

Nowadays we have more information on our hands compared to them and likewise we have a more complex thinking pattern. Obviously, it is an advanced thinking pattern given that we are supplied with more than one research article each day, filled with information about eating patterns, relationships, jobs, and so on.

The technological advancements and new social hierarchies introduced in the last 40 years does mean that the current generation has to train their minds to think faster, to absorb stress and feel joyful. After all, we are born to enjoy our life and not be stressed out all the time. However, the fast pace of our lives does not allow us to ponder on these things. We are forever tied to the plough, going round and around, digging the same old barren earth. I was doing the same till life struck me. It struck me hard and fast and I had no chance to stop and think, react and correct the course. When it was all over I was devastated. It took me a long time to understand that there is a beautiful life waiting for us to behold and live, provided that we know the secret to happiness. I have written this book to enlighten others who are going through similar experiences. Every one of you must read this book in order to lead a healthier, happier and successful life.

Who is this book for?

There is nothing religious about meditation and you do not have to chant anything. In fact, this is a scientifically proven technique widely used in psychology since 1970s to address depression, stress, anxiety and also addictions. Similar to other practices nothing comes easy. So, you have to put a bit of effort and very good focus and motivation levels and once you practice these there will definitely be rewards.

This book is not restricted to people in a certain profession or at a certain stage in their life. In fact, the earlier you adopt this in your life the better. Even if you are happy you can adopt meditation. There isn't a negative impact, meditation just prepares your mind to handle tough situations. There are times when you might feel that your body or mind is getting too distracted to continue. You have to believe this is normal. Rarely, can someone sit for the first time or the first few times and be able to focus without an ounce of distraction. Which is why no one should accept this as failure. Just remember that you are only sparing a few minutes a day and once you are able to focus the benefits are endless.

I would like to remind that this won't be a quick fix remedy type book. You have to put in the hard work and you need to focus mainly on what you want to achieve. If you are prepared to put in the hard work please proceed.

Note: I have used mindfulness and meditation interchangeably, because the meditation practices I have discussed are intended to improve your ability to be mindful.

Chapter 1 - Mind & Mindfulness

What is mind?

There is a logical sequence of events in an average person's life - school, college, university, work, love, marriage, kids, and retirement. Whether the person eventually works as a fireman, police officer, software engineer or a salesman who travels a lot, eventually life gives experiences that are unique to them. No two experiences are the same nor are the reaction to them. Every person reacts in a different way to similar experiences. These experiences are perceived by us through our mind. Oxford dictionary has the definition of mind as "The element of a person that enables them to be aware of the world and their experiences, to think, and to feel; the faculty of consciousness and thought - synonyms: brain, intelligence, intellect"[i].

However, in Buddhism the mind is not seen as synonymous to brain. Instead it is seen as a separate entity to the body, given that our body can go into a state of relaxation and sleep where as our mind can still be busy[ii]. To know more you can refer to the book 'Understanding the mind' by Geshe Kelsang Gyatso[iii].

The mind is not a static muscle. Each moment millions of electrical pulses are working through your brain to control every aspect of your being – from the most complex to the most mundane. Your brain is programmed to be in a constant state of work. Our aim, during meditation, is to know this and to channel this constant "state of work" to where we want it to go.

What is Mindfulness?

Simply put, Mindfulness is a state of mind where you live in the current moment and you can identify what's going on inside your mind every moment and therefore be in control of your thought process. Professor Mark Williams, former director of the Oxford Mindfulness Centre says "It's easy to stop noticing the world around us. It's also easy to lose touch with the way our bodies are feeling and to end up living 'in our heads' – caught up in our thoughts without stopping to notice how those thoughts are driving our emotions and behavior. An important part of mindfulness is reconnecting with our bodies and the sensations they experience. This means waking up to the sights, sounds, smells and tastes of the present moment. That might be something as simple as the feel of a banister as we walk upstairs. It's about allowing ourselves to see the present moment clearly. When we do that, it can positively change the way we see ourselves and our lives"[iv] .

In addition to the feeling of relaxation, it is a way to observe the patterns of our thoughts and how sometimes you can be consumed by them or get carried away, in turn distracting you from what you are doing in the present. Once we take a step back and notice them we can train ourselves to notice these thoughts, notice they are just a 'mental thought process' that do not have to control us. For example, consider a person is attending a key meeting where he or she is going to demo a product or an important exam or giving a lecture or a law enforcement officer in a pursuit. Their presence in the moment is absolutely needed to finish the task at hand. If you get entangled in a thought process right in the middle of it even for a split second you end up taking a pause trying to get back to the moment. Depending on the length of the pause, there is a high chance that they will either lose precious time or feel embarrassed because others notice the pause or in the case of a police officer they may lose sight of a dangerous criminal or endanger lives. I hope none of these situations ever happen to anyone however you have to be Mindful and be able to notice when your mind is unknowingly distracted onto something else. Many may be unaware that such a thing is happening. Even if they know most of them may treat it as granted saying 'mind can get distracted' and many more will be unaware that when it happens there is a way to avoid it.

Check your MOOD

In UK, the National Health Service provides a self-assessment questionnaire[v] to find out whether one has depression or anxiety. A low score indicates that there is a less chance of either of them or both. A high score obviously means you have to seek help. These days' mobile phones have health apps that can find out your stress level. If you do not have such device I have attached a few useful online tools that can help you. The tests themselves are free and some of these links either provide courses or ask you to pay for a personalized report but you don't have to. You can just take the free test and take a screenshot or print out.

- BeMindFulOnline.com Stress test [vi]
- Stress.org.uk [vii]

Note: - These are not my courses and I am not promoting the links.

Stress or Anxiety

Stress is actually needed for you. Believe me! It is a key survival instinct, it motivates to achieve your goals and be more efficient. It is your body responding to any threat or danger i.e. an automatic defense system called as 'fight-or-flight'. Walter Bradford Cannon, an American physiologist first explained this as a reaction by the nervous system in response to a perceived danger (even animals go through this). Our nervous system regulates the heart rate, digestion, sexual arousal, respiratory rate, urination and so on. The sympathetic nervous system that is responsible for releasing the stress hormones for the fight-or-flight response originates in the spinal cord. When this happens the heart pounds faster, blood pressure rises, muscles tighten and the breath quickens.

An article written on ulifeline.org says "Stress is a burst of energy that basically advises you on what to do. In small doses, stress has many advantages. For instance, stress can help you meet daily challenges and motivates you to reach your goals. In fact, stress can help you accomplish tasks more efficiently. It can even boost memory." Though stress is a natural instinct, it should not start dictating your life. You should not become a slave to stress. If it is affecting your daily life then you definitely need help. In most scenarios stress or anxiety is un-identifiable unless it manifests into something bad.

Benefits of meditation and mindfulness (physical, mental & spiritual)

Meditation is a practice that leads to a better physical, emotional and mental balance in a person. This in turn, leads to a lowering of anxiety and stress. This reduces chances of depression.

As medical science explains, a stressful situation triggers the sympathetic nervous system - launching the mind into a higher 'combat' mode – the classical 'flight or fight' response. This automatically releases adrenaline into the bloodstream, heightening the body's defense mechanism. As a result, blood pressure (and blood flow) increases, breathing shortens and the pulse rate increases. If the stress is not released, it constantly builds up and leaves a person feeling constantly stressed out; eventually leading to psychosomatic illnesses. This is a very common problem in today's fast and stressful lifestyles.

It has been found that meditation activates the parasympathetic nervous system. Blood flow is directed to the part of the brain that relaxes the mind and body, reduces the pulse rate and conserves energy. This is why meditation is being increasingly prescribed as a treatment to supplement (though not to replace) medicines for stress related disorders.

Meditation has helped people in diverse areas as – smoking addiction, overcoming drug and alcohol addiction, reducing blood pressure, reducing symptoms of pre-menstrual syndrome and menopause. People regularly practicing meditation also report increased emotional control, vitality and self-esteem.

There have been studies produced in the recent years using modern scientific techniques and instruments, such as fMRI and EEG into meditation. These techniques were used to directly observe brain physiology and neural activity in humans, either during the act of meditation itself, or before and after a meditation effort. This allowed the researchers to establish the link between the meditative practice and changes in brain structure or function.

According to researchers at Harvard, the number of randomized controlled trials — the gold standard for clinical study — involving mindfulness has jumped from one in the period from 1995–1997 to 11 from 2004–2006, to a whopping 216 from 2013–2015.

Here are some of the benefits split with meditation –

Olivia Smith

Health Benefits

Studies are starting to show how meditation has a positive effect on the health of the individual. Training your mind will have a direct impact on improving your body's health.

Healthy heart–Studies are starting to show that meditation might be one of many ways to reduce cholesterol and blood pressure. Any way to reduce cholesterol and blood pressure is of course a way to a healthier and happier heart.

Arthritis and other joint diseases –Meditation appears to have a direct impact on pain and stiffness associated with chronic pain disorders.

Fatigue and sleep disorders – People practicing meditation can get a bonus that transcends into every health category. Fatigue sets the stage for illness and stress if one cannot get a good night's sleep. Getting a good night's sleep will help fight off and recover from the disease. Those who meditate should find it easier to refocus the attention better and therefore find it easier to control i.e. to fall asleep and stay asleep.

Push away harmful stress – It not only provides physical health benefits; meditation is also a great way to prevent stress. Anyone who has ever practiced meditation can say very well that it helped him or her cope with stress.

Meditation has two advantages – one to provide a healthy body and the other to provide a healthy mind.

So yeah? Why don't we just try it starting now? You can and sometimes people do benefit immediately but most of the times it takes time to find the right technique. As I have covered in the introduction, there are hundreds of meditation techniques and that's why it's better to follow someone who has gone through the same path and use their advice to get to your goal much quicker.

Who can perform meditation?

There is a misconception about who can practice meditation. I have seen people claiming that it is for the old. Nothing can be far from the truth. In fact, I advise youngsters to take up meditation at the earliest – earlier the better. Parents can initiate children to this wonderful technique by including the practices in their games. Children learn faster when they look at it like a game. It's a good idea not to force anything on the children because they tend to hate anything which is thrust upon them. Introducing breathing techniques to them can be beneficial but do it in a playful way, by creating a comfortable environment, choosing a calmer time when they are not busy with other activities. There are plenty of techniques to teach for children which would take a whole new book.

That being said, you can begin meditating at any age.

Kids
Teens,
Young adults,
Adults and
Seniors

Everyone can learn to meditate. The only question is which technique to choose. The techniques discussed in this book are simple however, as I said earlier, be playful with the kids. Choose the one you and they are the most comfortable with. Remember, that you do not need an 'innate ability' to meditate. All you need is to put a little effort. If you need help, hopefully, this book will give you the gentle nudge that's needed.

Why isn't everyone doing it?

This is a good question. To be honest, I would ask the same question i.e. why isn't everyone taking up meditation. This question is for people who do not do it. If meditation is so good for your wellbeing, why isn't everyone doing it?

I struggle to answer this question myself sometimes. As someone, who is on the other side of the road maybe I have seen the path and also what's on the other side and therefore it is sometimes baffling – maybe I can help you – do you want to take the first step.

Let's be honest though why would someone take up the offer? In my childhood I have not dreamt myself about taking up meditation. Why? Simplistically, I did not know about it and even if I knew it's boring. Yes, it's boring to sit and be still – I want to stay active – I want to may be listen to music – I want to watch TV – I want to watch a comedy episode on YouTube – I want to go to gym and workout – I want to play football or cricket.

None of them are wrong. Why? The reason is everyone has a zone where they want to go back to at the sign of trouble – remember the 'fight-or-flight' response? It's also true that we are always looking for entertainment and usually are attracted to people who can entertain themselves well. Any of these activities are better than sitting and thinking about whatever caused you stress. If a couple is in an argument, they may think that they can argue their way out of it, because the other person may understand and that solves it. However, it may not always work out like that. If at least one of them has some activity to fall back to, whether its gym, music etc. it would help them refocus their thoughts and turn back to what's really important. Without this 'self-centered' activity it would be difficult for that person to reduce their stress levels.

So, now, when you hear someone say, music helped me refocus on what's important in life, you know what they mean. Is this similar to meditation? My answer is yes and no. There are people who would stay on the strong side of 'yes' and others who stay on the strong side of 'no'. I am one of those who would say it's 50/50. Let me cover what I mean.

Simplistically, you need to stick to whatever works for you.

I am not here to sell you Meditation but I am here to give you the insights into it to help you make the choice. Meditation is a great tool that will help you take control of your thoughts and in turn life by using simple methods and simple activities one does in their daily life. Depending on the type of technique you choose, the benefit varies. They all may seem similar though at first i.e. they all could be focused on breathing but they are not all the same. There will be subtle differences. In photography, two people can go to the same beautiful sunrise location, at the same time and come back with two completely different images. Assuming their creative levels are the same the difference in result could have been because they used different technique – for example, one used wide landscape lens and the other used telephoto lens. Similarly, in meditation the technique you choose gives you different results. Your goal might also be different. If, your primary goal was to refocus your mind back to what's important and if you are already tuned to an activity such as music or gym etc., then meditation will give you similar result so it's better to stick to what you are already doing.

However, the 'no' part comes where meditation will continue to help you in the background once you have practiced it enough. The other activities may not be realistic always, as you need to physically perform those activities to refocus. Meditation will take time. But the more you practice the better the result. If, in daily life, you are having to constantly revert back to those activities, it's not always practical to do them, as you may be unable to start the activity due a practical situation i.e. you may have an important meeting or something similar. It might also mean that you have to rethink about the root cause of those stressful situations in the first place, as may be changing jobs is better for you or the relationship does not work anymore. However, these are out of the scope of this book. Alternatively, meditation once it's practiced enough will help you in the background.

If you can take 15 seconds to breath and relax in a mindful meditative manner or if you have practiced meditation enough that you can separate out stressful thought and focus on the options to eradicate it or address the criticality of that situation, that would be super cool. You will be surprised at the fast rate at which your mind is able calculate and adjust your thoughts and feelings. It can separate out the emotions, positive thoughts, and negative thoughts and evaluate the options and the impacts of each of the options. Whether the impact is to assess the feelings of the people in front of you or the deadline of a project or the budget of a project etc. Once you reach this stage there is no going back. This is when you really start reaping the benefits of meditation.

Beginner's dilemma

Now that we have covered the benefits of meditation and who can mediate and also why do you need to meditate, let's look at the common beginner's dilemma. As with anything in life most people experience a dilemma. The dilemma could be

a)   I have doubts on whether I should practice it or not
b)   I have doubts on which technique should be used

Let's cover these one by one.

I have doubts on whether I should practice it or not

Here are the common misconceptions I have heard of.

- The practice is related to Hindu or Buddhist religion
- Why does breathing make a difference
- I cannot stop the flow of thoughts
- I don't have time
- It's boring
- I don't want to place restrictions on food
- There are too many techniques. The choice confuses me

Now let's address each topic one by one –

The practice is related to Hindu or Buddhist religion – Some think that since it is related to Hindu and Buddhist religion, they would have to convert to those religions. This is not true. Meditation or Mindfulness may have its origin in Eastern philosophy but is now a scientifically proven technique and you are free to profess any religion while practicing meditation.

Why does breathing make a difference – This is a common question. "I breathe everyday but what difference does it make by doing another breathing exercise." The answer is that mindfulness breathing is more than just a breathing exercise. Remember the photography example where two people go to the same spot but come out with different results. The one difference was technique. Meditation is similar – there are many techniques which provide different results. Meditation uses breathing in a way that helps the body and mind. If meditation was just breathing there would not be paid meditation classes in almost every town or gym. I will cover more on this in Chapter 3.

I cannot stop the flow of thoughts – Many beginners feel that they are not able to be mindful because they cannot stop the flow of random thoughts. This is absolutely normal. There is a technique in mindfulness where instead of bringing back the focus to your breathing you can simply watch the thoughts – however you have to do this in a detached manner – not reacting or becoming involved with the thoughts, worries or memories. So, the flow of thoughts is not a failure. If in 'concentrative' meditation, one has to gently nudge the mind back to the object of concentration. With 'mindfulness' meditation, one has to simply watch the thoughts in a detached manner – not reacting or becoming involved with the thoughts, worries or memories.

I don't have time – The other concern of a beginner is the time to be spent on meditation. Most people say that they do not have time. My experience shows that about 10 minutes each in the morning or evening is more than adequate which I am sure is less than the time to go through Facebook posts or Newspaper or twitter etc.

The ideal times would be early in the morning after getting up or late at night before going to sleep. You may, in fact, start with just 5 minute sessions and gradually increase to a 10-minute regime. The next topic 'when to meditate' gives you in detail a clear breakdown of the different times of the day you can choose to meditate.

It's boring – We have covered on this topic in the previous section. I wouldn't argue on this though that initially it would seem boring but the *long term benefits outweigh the short term feelings*. Remember, the benefits and what you can achieve in life with them. Be positive. Think positive.

I don't want to place restrictions on food - Does one have to give up many types of food (or become a vegetarian) to be able to meditate successfully? The answer is simply No. Meditation does not impose any special dietary restrictions. However, what would be preferable is to be comfortable when doing meditation. This also means that if you have a heavy meal before meditation it's of little benefit as ideally it's better to leave your body to digest food. You can however choose to meditate just before a meal.

There are too many techniques. The choice confuses me – You might find it surprising but this is the one reason why most people procrastinate. Yes, the choice of techniques is daunting. This is why I will be covering the key techniques in this book. If you know of a technique but don't find it in this book – I would advise try practicing the techniques in this book first as for most these would be sufficient. If you want to learn about other practices and other topics such as yoga and stress management then go to theyogamastery.com. If you would prefer a book in any of the topics drop me an email (by subscribing on booklisher.com).

This leads us on to the next dilemma.

I have doubts on which technique should be used

Choosing the type of meditation technique is the beginner's first predicament – *a piquant situation of 'stress' arising in selecting a stress-reduction method!*

I feel that you must choose a method that suits you the best. However, in the absence of experience, it is advisable to opt for a 'Concentration' technique based on breathing. Breathing is a natural and readily available object of meditation. As one improves in concentration, one can gradually try out other meditation techniques. The 'Concentration' technique involves sitting or lying in a calm place in a position you are comfortable in and observing the inhalation and exhalation. When the mind gets distracted bring it back gently to the present moment and focus on your breathing. The other techniques discussed in chapter 3 and 4 are very simple and you can choose any of these and do not bother about any other techniques.

When to Meditate?

Once you've decided to invest your time and effort in learning how to meditate, you also need to decide when and how to meditate. Let's cover the when part here. Just remember that meditation brings many benefits in areas such as health, concentration, stress, anxiety and joy. It's important that we do not stress about when to meditate, so take this section as a guide to help you take that step.

If you aren't feeling at ease yet – let me just say that – all it takes is 5 minutes in a day.

There are 24 hours i.e. 1440 minutes in a single day so let's split this out -

- The recommended sleeping time is between 6 to 8 hours a day. So, considering a max of 8 hours if we subtract these minutes out you will have (1440 − (8 * 60)) = 960. From these remaining 960 minutes now we need to pick 5 minutes.

- Now let's say you work from 9 to 5 and it's not a work from home so you have to travel to office. This will take away another 480 minutes out considering an hour of travel each way – to and from office. This leaves you with 480 minutes. Note – just so you know you can also pick time in your office as well. I will cover on this later in the book.

- Considering you can't find time during office hours, can you think of the time in these remaining 480 minutes where you can choose 5 minutes? Let me help you with this –

  - *Do you go to gym?*
    - Most gyms have meditation and yoga classes. Find out about them. Note that most of the classes are not included in the gym membership so you may have to pay extra.

- If you prefer to do it on your own using the techniques in this book (which is what I would recommend) then you can find a quiet spot in the gym or preferably what I would recommend is find a quiet spot at your home before the gym.

o *Do you wake up at 10 mins or 15 mins or 30 mins or even an hour before you travel to office?*

- Studies have shown that morning fatigue could be caused by over sleeping and not having enough time for your body to feel fully awake. Sometimes people throw in one or two strong coffee to get rid of the morning fatigue. This will only make things worse in the long term as you are throwing all this extra caffeine into your body.

- Ideally, studies have shown that waking up early have had proven benefits both mentally and physically. So, if you can try waking up early at 6am or even 5am, then, you will, for sure have a chance to spare more than 5 mins (assuming your work day does not start that early). Ideal time is early morning before you are fully awakened to the daily stress activities. I would recommend taking a shower. If you can't then I would recommend at-least sprinkling water on your face just after you brush your teeth. This should be enough to get you started. I will cover more on the preparation part in chapter 3.

o *What? 5am? No, I cannot do that. I am not an early riser – what can I do.* I can understand this as well as I have a few friends who aren't early risers. Let's assume in that case then most of the morning is gone in preparing lunch or breakfast and getting ready and dropping of kids if you are married or taking care of adults in case you live with your parents.

- Ideally, since you only need 5 minutes you can think of waking up possibly 10 minutes before your normal wake up and take 5 mins to prepare and 5 minutes to practice meditation.

- It's possible that your work hours actually start early so you genuinely do not have time in the morning. In this case there are other opportunities we can easily find in your evening schedule.
- *Blow off the steam* – Raise your hands if you take a relaxing breath just after you reach home after a hard day at work. Normally, you would ease yourself into home by taking a shower or washing your face and then putting on loose clothes. This is the perfect opportunity to extend this routine to a few more minutes and practice meditation. This will help you blow off any steam left from the daily stress at workplace or the travel.
- If you cannot do this then there are other opportunities. *If you prepare meals once you reach home* then this is an awesome opportunity. Most cooking will need some amount of boiling on the stove or baking in oven etc. Can you use this time where you know you don't need to attend to cooking to practice meditation?
- *Do you watch TV once you reach home?* Well you may know where I will go now isn't it. You guessed right, why don't you reduce the TV watching time by 5 mins?
- *Have you thought of a family meditation time?* Yes, this is a real thing. If you know something will benefit you don't you want your family to benefit too? Yes, you would definitely want them to benefit too. Between us, this will help them not distract you as well especially if you have noisy kids. There are plenty of fun practices for you to follow. Please drop in your email address on the website BookLisher.com and let me know if you want to learn about these practices. Back onto our topic, you can choose to have a family meditation time by inviting everyone to take part and creating a fun filled environment. Studies have shown that similar to group therapies, group meditation is a brilliant way to create an environment where each participant is motivated by another and you can also engage later by talking about each other's experiences

during the meditation. Sometimes, learning from these experiences can add new perspective to the way you practice daily. Also, equally beneficial factor in this is engaging with each other in getting ready to meditate could be a fun time and usually fun times lead to happy moments and as you know if you are happy your mind is in very pleasant state, helping you to achieve your goal in meditation much quicker.

- *Did you know that you can meditate just before sleeping in bed?* Yes, that's true. Sleep meditation is one form of meditation where you practice meditation while you are in sleep position on your bed or on the floor. More on this will be covered in the chapter 4. You can also take the usual seating position just before you go to bed as part of your 'getting ready to sleep' routine.

- *If you still haven't found the slot – read on - Do you spend half hour in the loo looking at your tablet or phone?* I know for many people this is their thinking time as well i.e. to browse for ideas/shopping/relationship advice on internet that you normally won't get time for outside due to the busy schedules. This is one place no one cares to disturb you.

    - If you do this then you, technically, have already started taking time for yourself so why not shave 5 or 10 minutes out of the loo time and use it to practice meditation? Obviously, not saying you should do it in the loo – I meant after you finish with your loo.

- Other ideas ...
    - People run or cycle during office lunch hours to keep fit. Can you do a similar thing by sparing a few minutes to practice meditation? If anything this will reduce any stress built up during the day as well and will refocus back on whatever you want to.
    - *Meditate on the train or bus?* This may feel a bit extreme but no it isn't. There is no reason to feel embarrassed as well. I see people sleep on the train or bus all the time. *All you need to do is the same thing as these people, just that you are not actually sleeping. You have your eyes*

closed and are observing your breath and thoughts. You are just being mindful of your own self...

- *Do you walk to office?* You can take a mindfulness walk. This practice is not in scope of this book but is covered on the website theyogamastery.com.
- *Do you like gardening?* Gardening in itself is an excellent stress buster. Just imagine the pleasant smells and the water droplets on the petals of the plants. If you have a chance I would prefer to practice meditation in these serene surroundings. You can use DIY tools or hire someone to build yourself a small area for you to sit – may be a bench, or a little shed or little wooden platform. If nothing else works out just take a bedsheet and lay it on the grass and sit on it. I do that all the time and it works perfectly.
- *Do you live by the beach or a hill or a park?* If you live close to any of these places then take an early morning stroll. If you are lucky you may catch the sunrise. Early morning sunrays are supposed to be very good for your skin as well so take the additional benefits while you can.

How often should you meditate?

The first and the most important aspect of beginning meditation is committing yourself wholeheartedly from the outset. The words 'I think', 'I believe', 'I will try' convey doubt in the approach and will not indulge confidence. When you convey to others about meditation make sure you speak confidently that you will for sure meditate.

When one starts meditating, it may not be easy to concentrate and therefore it would be difficult getting your focus right. This might affect the confidence in meditation itself. Didn't I say already that the mind's mischievous habit is to get distracted? Which is why it is important to keep in mind that when you first begin to meditate, keep your expectations in check. Start off slowly and gradually increase the time. In this way, you won't start off with too many expectations and therefore you won't get disappointed. Give it some time.

Start off with 5-minute intervals each morning. Remember what I said earlier about sparing at least another 5 minutes for preparation. Morning is best because your body hasn't fully awakened yet to the day to day stress activities. Thereafter, when you begin to see the rewards of meditation, you can increase and adjust your schedule accordingly.

Do not expect to be miraculously transformed in the beginning. Meditation - just like anything else - takes time, patience, and practice.

Chapter 2 – Meditation & Mindfulness

When I questioned people about what they think about mindfulness I received varied responses. Some find mindfulness to be a difficult task. At the other end of the spectrum, some think it is as easy as eating a cake. Who is right? I suppose both opinions are right if you are looking at mindfulness as an outsider who has never practiced mindfulness before. To find out the exact nature of mindfulness, the obvious solution is to become mindful. Can you focus on your immediate actions for five minutes? If you can be mindful, for even a few minutes, you are already practicing mindfulness. There are some other aspects of mindfulness which you must consider before declaring yourself a master of mindfulness. It is far easier to be calm and composed in happy situations. The real test comes when you have to be mindful when the world around you is falling apart. To cut it short, being mindful is not easy. You have to practice mindfulness. Also, there is a process which you must adopt to become mindful. You just can't reach your goal in a haphazard manner. Thankfully, there are many ways to reach your goal of mindfulness. Meditation is one of them.

If you are getting alarmed at the mention of meditation, don't. Meditation is not as complicated and time consuming as some people lead us to believe. Television and media have ingrained us to believe that the way to properly meditate is to sit in a seemingly impossible body positions for hours on end. You don't have to have a flexible body, you need not own a retreat in the mountains, and you do not even need a membership to a fancy Zen spa. All you need is quiet place where you will not be disturbed and a willingness to learn. I cannot promise you fame and fortune if you start to meditate, but what I will promise is to try and reconnect you to yourself. The practice of meditating will transform your life. You will gain a deeper appreciation of yourself and your world.

HOW TO MEDITATE?

Even if you've tried to meditate in the past and stopped, this book is designed to break through all the barriers which have kept you from meditating. This program is designed to use these age old traditions and make them current to today's lifestyle. My goal in creating this system is to make meditations easy to understand, flexible enough to be done every day without hindering your daily routine. Meditation will bring clarity of mind, a feeling of wellbeing, a sense of control and ultimately an inner contentment and happiness.

Before we start let's set aside all those disempowering excuses why you can't meditate. I have heard them all. 'I don't have time in my day.' 'Seems too complicated.' I am here to tell you that everyone can learn to mediate, not matter what life circumstance you're in. You've already proven to yourself that you want to learn to meditate by getting this program, so leave all the excuses why you can't meditate aside and just relax and enjoy.

Most people are so busy getting through life they forget to live. Meditation is about getting your awareness to the present moment. Most of the time our thoughts are in the past – what could I have done – or in the future – what will I be doing. Meditation refocuses the mind to think and be in the present moment. Your whole life is made up of moments that you experience in the present tense. Your life is the sum of all those moments. So if you're living your life in other than the present moment then you are missing out on life. The sight of a new born baby – the beauty of a sunset – the beauty of summer rain – People are too involved with where they are going and where they came from and because of it they are missing out on where they are.

Meditation is about being in the present moment. From this we can lay the foundation on how to meditate.

The brains thought process is random and chaotic jumping from subject to subject very rapidly. It follows an age old saying – ask someone not to think of pink elephants and that's exactly what the person will think of. The brain has no choice.

Focusing you attention to your breathing, forces your brain to have a resting place of thought, a constant state and not jumping around.

Living in the moment – from moment to moment

Find the joy of every moment by being in the moment and you will finally be able to enjoy them. *Even in the most mundane circumstances, you can live a richer life just by being in the moment.* Life's simple pleasures jump out at you once again. Here's a simple example – putting away the laundry – feel the crispness of the fabric in your hands – smell the freshness – see how the light dances on the surface – feel the satisfaction of a job well done.

Carry meditation though your whole day by being aware of what the mind is thinking and being able to direct the mind to the present. If all else fails focus the mind on your breathing to bring you back to the present.

Meditation will free you from the negative thoughts and lets you take control. It's a way for you to discover about yourself, what makes you happy, what makes you sad and puts the power of choice in your own hands to attain what you want.

Meditation is simply a training of the mind, not thinking chaotically but by focusing on the one thing that grounds a person to the present – breathing. If all this seem confusing, just wait for a few more minutes. In the following chapters I will dwell deeper in the process and types of mindfulness techniques to derive joy and happiness from your everyday life.

What Happens During Meditation?

Normally, you won't find a traditional doctor who will prescribe just meditation as the sole means of healing your illness. Yet, meditation is something about which doctors tell you in other ways.

For example, how often did your doctor tell you that stress was a health problem? Or, maybe he told you that you need to relax more so you can overcome your headaches, your pain or your tension? In other words, your doctor is encouraging you to clear your mind about the things you worry about and concentrate instead on relaxation.

However, the mechanics behind how meditation works is quite different. Not many realize how meditation actually works or why does it matter that they know why it works. Let's take a look at both how and why here.

HOW TO MEDITATE?

There is evidence in recent studies that meditation can produce a reaction in a body. Recent studies have shown that people who meditated for an eight-week period had shown effect on genes and helped regulate glucose metabolism, blood pressure, inflammation. A further research using fMRI, showing activation in the amygdala where the patients under study were asked to watch emotional content before learning meditation. After eight weeks of training in mindful attention the researchers observed that amygdala was less activated. There are still vast scale researches going on, but the results so far look positive.

Following list is about what goes on in your body during meditation.

1. Your breathing becomes regulated, smoother and deeper.

2. It helps regulate the amount of the stress hormone, called plasma cortisol that is produced by your body.

3. Your heart rate decreases, which means that your heart beats slower.

4. You will feel relaxed due to increase in brain wave stimulation. This is called your EEG or electroencephalograph alpha that is directly related to the ability of the body to relax.

5. It can lower your pulse rate

6. Your body will exhibit a decrease in the metabolic rate. This is probably the most astonishing physical experience.

It's not just physical changes that happen during meditation. The body enters a state of relaxation and rest that is not possible through any other practice.

Your mind and brain are extremely alert and in tune during this time. As described above, the medical experiments conducted prove the changes in activity.

Chapter 3 - How to perform mindfulness

Normally our mind works like a machine. It's working 24/7. It is in constant motion of thinking, feeling, flitting from one thought to another endlessly. Due to this continuous motion the mind becomes tired, dull and slow. Awareness may peep through all this but the negative thoughts are higher and they simply subdue the awareness. Noisy thoughts and gloomy emotions cloud our thinking and we land up in a mess. You become edgy and upset without any reason. Anger peeps in and when you're angry there is no room for happiness. This is when you need to practice mindfulness. Where there is mindfulness there is peace, calm and joy. You're completely aware of what is happening. This awareness helps you to shed the negative thoughts and your mind finds balance.

As with any meditation session, you need to get into a relaxed and comfortable position, eyes closed, and then commence with deep nasal breathing, focusing your thoughts on the breathing to ease yourself into a meditative state. Once you feel that you are calm and that your breath is under your rhythmic control, then you can move on to focusing on your own body, a part at a time. There are four steps to practice mindfulness. They are preparation, relaxation, mindfulness and stillness.

Step 1 - Preparation
Step 2 - Relaxation
Step 3 - Mindfulness
Step 4 – Stillness

HOW TO MEDITATE?

Step 1 - Preparation

Preparation is about all the practical details of posture, place and time to meditate, attitude and how to begin your meditation practice.

Place of meditation

Choose a place in your home where you feel comfortable. Meditate at the same place every day. It shouldn't be that you keep changing your place of meditation. So select a favorite corner where you particularly feel comfortable and sit there every day. You can also meditate out in the open. By the sea or on top of a mountain or in your neighborhood garden where you've chirping birds and waves for company. Your mind automatically gets calm and serene. Peaceful surroundings are essential for practicing any form of meditation, especially mindfulness. The endeavor is to create a space in your home or outside where you can feel safe and secure to meditate in peace. It'll be your 'go to' place, away from the outside world where you can introspect and shed all your unnecessary and unwanted thoughts. This place will help you to heal, grow and bloom into a positive, calm and satisfied person. Some people are lucky to have a separate room for meditating but it's not mandatory. The key thing is keep that space de-cluttered. You can have an aromatic candle and a vase with flowers or whatever makes you feel comfortable as you need the place to be welcoming. Keep it as your meditation space so that the moment you enter the room peace engulfs you. There are many ways of making the approach to meditation as joyful as possible. You can transform the most ordinary of rooms into an intimate sacred space, an environment where every day you go to meet with your true self with all the joy and happy habit of one old friend greeting another.

What do you wear?

Another aspect in preparation is the clothes you wear. Avoid wearing tight fit clothes while meditating. Wear loose clothes that will help you to sit in peace for a while. Formal clothes and jeans are a definite no, no. Remember mindfulness is all about breathing. So wear clothes that you're comfortable to breathe in. Another aspect is a mat to sit on. Instead of sitting on your bed or sofa, it'll be ideal to squat on the floor on top of a mat.

Posture

Posture is important in mindfulness meditation so that the energy will flow better. Sit in a comfortable posture. Sitting cross legged with hands on the knees (Padmasana/Lotus pose) is perfect for meditation. The spine is straight and the back is erect. Your head looks ahead and hands are stretched. This position helps to concentrate on a single object while meditating as your body is balanced. Mindfulness is about concentrating on your breathing. Some meditation techniques also suggest sitting in a comfortable position in a chair as well if you cannot sit down. Whether you sit up or lie down the aim is to have symmetry in your posture so that your body is balanced on both sides.

> *Jenny, a banker was totally stressed after a hard day at work. Meeting clients, managing funds, reaching targets put a lot of responsibility on her thin shoulders. She had constant headaches and lack of sleep till one of her colleagues mentioned about mindfulness to her. She met with a Guru and learnt to meditate. After a couple of months Jenny decided to meditate every day at home. She selected the smaller room as meditation room in her swanky 2 BHK apartment. She kept a chair and a small center table in that room. She used her grandmother's crochet table cloth for that center table. She kept a crystal candle stick above it which was also heirloom. The table cloth and candle stick made her nostalgic and reminded her of the love and wonderful times she shared with her grandmother. She also had a yoga mat and a vase in one corner. She refilled the vase once in two days with fresh flowers. Her meditation room gave her inner peace as soon as she entered the room, as it transported her to the days she spent in loving care of her grandmother. The room more or less became a holy place to Jenny. Whenever she thought of her room there was a smile on her face. The fact that she had a meditation room where she could connect with her pleasant past and remain peaceful made her rush back home every day.*

Jenny lighted the candle everyday as she sat down to meditate. The glow from the candle gave her peace and the room was tranquil with the glowing candle and fresh flowers. This room made her feel good and she looked forward to her meditation routine. When you start your day in such a peaceful atmosphere you can enter the mindfulness state quicker.

Step 2 - Relaxation

Relaxation has everything to do with your mind and body. Now that you've established a regular place to meditate you've think about how to relax both your body and mind. Tell yourself that you're going to be fine and all your problems will be solved and you'll be free from worries. As you tell this to yourself you'll feel the tension leaving your body and you feel relaxed. As your mind is calm it becomes clearer and you're able to assess your situation with clarity. You let go of unwanted thoughts and think about the now. When you're relaxing you need to be aware of where you're and in which posture you're. Slowly tell yourself to relax each and every part of your body. Here it is important to mention that you can keep your eyes closed. Start from your feet and move upwards to each and every part of your body. From feet you move to your legs then thighs, hips, hands, fingers, shoulders and then move upwards to your face. This is known as progressive muscle relaxation (PMR) exercise. Ask yourself how your body is feeling today? Are your feet fine? Is your hip aching? Here it is important to be positive. Relax into relaxation and be content to notice how your body is feeling today.

Let go of all expectations during this exercise. The aim of this exercise is to perform without any judgment. This way your body will also respond positively to your mind. The PMR exercise makes you aware of each and every part of your body that'll help you to relax and enjoy this journey. Our mission is to relax the body that automatically calms the mind and takes you into the meditative state where you're fully mindful (aware) of yourself. Once you reach this state of relaxation the body and mind are in balance with each other.

The secret is to assume an open interest as to how your body feels at that particular moment, as you're performing this exercise and to accept that this is the truth of the matter, this is how it is, and then to use these techniques to lead your body into a deeper, more serene and relaxed state. The truth is it actually works. It's simple and direct. You spend 10 to 15 seconds on a specific part of your body and know how it feels and then move on to the next part to explore a different sensation. Your curiosity to know how each part of your body feels makes you to think about each and every part and that mindfulness (awareness) aids in relaxation.

When you're thinking about your muscles they contract and make you aware that you're thinking about them. For example, if you're thinking about your calf muscle then it automatically contracts and your mind helps you to identify that particular muscle group. Then you command your mind to relax it. This way you contract and relax each and every muscle in your body. While doing this you deliberately contract and relax the muscle there by removing the tension present in it. You'll notice that the muscle is softening and the tension created is going away. While releasing, the left over tension also leaves the body and you relax completely. Once this exercise of contracting, relaxing and then 'letting go' of the tension becomes a habit, you automatically 'let go' of tension while not meditating also.

> *When Rich was given the pink slip he thought his whole world had come to a standstill. His beautiful wife Rihanna and his two wonderful kids, his faithful dog came into his mental picture. How am I going to protect them all? How am I going to pay the mortgage, car loan and other bills? He could feel his blood pressure shooting up. Since he was regularly into meditation he simply pushed away such thoughts and relaxed himself by letting go of these thoughts. Quietly he left office and reached home and went straight into his meditation room. Soon he felt the familiar feeling of security engulf him as he entered his favorite abode. Instinctively he knew he'll survive this. He sat in his favorite chair and took the shawl and spread it on his legs, as he always did. He felt 'at home' and peaceful. He meditated for a while. During this he was able to relax and bring attention back to himself. In a circumstance when it's hard to think clear, due to meditation it was now possible to have a clear mind. After the meditation he refocused the attention back to himself and tried to focus on what is he good at and thought why not provide become a freelancer in his profession.*

Instead of fretting and stressing himself as well as his family Rich meditated and kept himself composed. He was also positive that something wonderful is sure to happen. He intuitively knew that he would succeed if he kept his calm and remain grounded. Meditation increases the level of intuition in the individual. If you are just starting off it may be difficult to achieve the same level of result with meditation. Therefore, you need make it your goal to practice it daily.

Step 3 - Mindfulness

Mindfulness is the third step where you're aware of your thoughts. It makes you mindful of your surroundings as well as your inner thoughts. Once your body is relaxed after preparation and relaxation you become aware of your thoughts. Mindfulness is like waking up to life. When you're in an agitated state you forget to look around you or think with clarity. A mindless life becomes dull and chaotic. With the practice of mindfulness you'll start to notice these things and learn to enjoy the simple pleasures of life.

Mindfulness develops attention, concentration and the ability to simply be present with little or no future, past or goal orientation. Mindfulness practice slows down the forward projection of the thinking mind, which is overly committed to achieving, getting, having, holding and protecting. Mindfulness practice slows down the momentum of the ego or the personality, and allows contact with a deeper, stiller, quieter part of one's true nature.

Breath is the bridge between your body and mind

The basic principle of mindfulness is attention to breathing. Our breath is what keeps us alive on this planet. There is no need to change your breathing pattern. Simply observe it. This is not a breathing exercise. The aim is to be aware of your breath rather than controlling it. Breath is what keeps us alive. That is why it is called 'Prana' in Sanskrit which means life's force. If there is no *prana* then the body is just a corpse. It is *prana* that keeps us alive. So you need to concentrate on your breathing. No need to alter it. Simply observe your breath. Be aware of how the air is inhaled and exhaled. Concentrate on the place above the upper lip and below the nostrils. You can feel the cold air entering your nostrils. When you exhale you'll feel the hot air coming out. This heat is generated by your body and this is energy. The cold air gets converted inside you to propel your body parts to be in optimum shape. While breathing, you'll feel your stomach and chest muscles contract and release. Listen to the rhythmic feel of your breath as it is the essential life giver for growth. Attention to the breath can produce a deep respect and appreciation for the breath of life.

If you feel that your thoughts are wandering away from your breath, gently bring it back to concentrate on your breathing. This will help you to relax and be mindful of your surroundings and inner self as well. You're free of judgment and free of reaction. In doing so you're able to think with rationality and mainly about those that helps you in achieving success. This is a very simple process where the effects are powerful.

Step 4 – Stillness

Stillness - As we become more mindful, we learn to give our attention more fully to whatever we are doing in the present moment, we notice a fundamental truth: there is activity in our life and there is stillness. Once you've prepared yourself for relaxing and being mindful of your breath, your body and mind are in balance with each other. Now you should try to control your thoughts. When mind is still then there is bliss, joy and satisfaction. Controlling your thoughts is a very essential part of mindfulness. You become nonjudgmental and focus completely on what you're doing. You can also remain still in the mind with a room full of people. If you can disassociate your thoughts from your surroundings then you can achieve stillness. Controlling your thoughts and training them to think what you want to is the ultimate aim of stillness. With continuous practice of meditation and mindfulness you achieve the state of stillness.

Start by concentrating on each and every body part one by one. By doing this you become aware of yourself. Once you've focused on each part of your body right leg, right knee, right hand, fingers, right eye, right ear and then move on to the left side. Now open your eyes and focus on a single object in the room. It can be anything like a flower vase or pen stand. Try to focus on it for half a minute and then turn away. While doing this keep your concentration on your breathing and your body parts. This triple focus makes you aware of your own self, your breathing and your surroundings. You can use an audio cd to guide you through this.

You may take up meditation to manage stress or to heal physically and mentally, to find more peace and balance in your life, to be more efficient at work or to perform better at sport, or to be a nicer person. All these things are real possibilities as a consequence of regular meditation, and it makes good sense to begin meditation with any of these intentions in mind. But the reason why meditation is the greatest gift you can give yourself—or, if you can, give to your loved one —is that meditation introduces us to our innermost nature, the truth of who we really are. You look within yourself and ask the question 'Who am I?' You will find answers to questions that've been plaguing you for a long time.

Resistance to meditate

Some people sleep during meditation. This is a form of resistance in our brain. The mind is continuously planning, plotting, judging, worrying and doesn't wish to be still. But with the practice of meditation you'll reach the state of calm and nothingness. While initially practicing meditation/mindfulness you may have unwanted thoughts entering your mind and refusing to go away. This is quite natural. *Look at your thoughts as if it is happening to someone else and learn to push it away.* With practice you'll be able to push away your thoughts and reach a state of peace.

Chapter 4 – Other Meditation Techniques

In the previous chapter, I took you through the process of mindfulness. I have discovered during my journey through mindfulness that there are some highly effective meditation techniques which can propel you faster to reach your goal. Obviously, there are many ways to train your mind and to remain mindful. As much as you, as an individual, you may prefer a particular technique to train the mind. I have already discussed breathing as a gateway to mindfulness. However, there are other powerful techniques which you may like to consider. You may follow any meditation technique that you are comfortable with. The choice is entirely yours. No one technique is better than the other. You can also combine two or more meditation practices. The important thing is that you must be comfortable doing them.

- **Yoga Nidra**
- **Anter Maun**
- **Transcendental Meditation**
- **Guided Meditation**
- **Body scan meditation**
- **Metta or loving kindness**

By now you must have realized that mindfulness is about awareness. You can't become aware unless you understand the resolve the interplay of your senses and mind. Instead of getting distracted by your senses, you must detach yourself from your senses through a process.

Here I will briefly discuss two important meditation practices first – Yoga Nidra (Psychic sleep) and Anter Maun (Inner silence). Besides these, I'll also take a look at transcendental meditation, guided meditation, Buddhist meditation, body scan and loving kindness meditation.

Anter Maun or Inner Silence

In this method, the practitioner is required to sit in an erect position, either in a lotus posture on the floor or on a firm surface. The spine must be in line with the head. The shoulders and body must remain calm and relaxed. The practitioner must become motionless. The eyes must be gently closed.

In the first stage of Anter Maun, one must become aware of the external stimuli like sounds, itching, smell and taste. The five sense organs are the eye, ear, nose, tongue and skin while the object of these senses are vision, sound, smell, taste and touch. One must observe all the sensations which are felt by the body through these sense organs. There should not be any reaction to any of the stimuli.

First one must concentrate on the various sounds around them. In the next step one must imagine that the ear is a person who is listening to another person which is the sound. The third person is the practitioner who must act as a witness to this conversation between two people. This position as a dispassionate observer or witness allows the person to be unaffected by the sound experienced by the ear. In a few minutes the practitioner will feel calm and peaceful. If you are unable to do this in your first few attempts don't be disheartened – I was in the same boat.

The second part of Anter Maun consists of turning the mind to the thoughts. Thoughts are creations of the mind and do not form due to any other reason. Thoughts must be allowed to come one by one without interruption. These thoughts may be anything – from the latest movie or experience, of fear, anger or happiness. One must watch the thoughts carefully and let them go. Observation of thoughts is critical. This in the Western world is called mindfulness. The practitioner is mindful of the thought processes and monitors them carefully.

In the final stage of Anter Maun, the practitioner must take control of the thoughts. Once a thought comes to the mind, stay with it for some time. One must treat the thoughts as a person and the mind as another person with both in conversation. The practitioner must look and observe the thoughts as an observer or a witness, without interfering with the natural flow of thoughts. One must willfully and consciously pick a specific thought, let it flow through the mind for some time and remove the thought. This process is repeated several times. The meditator will experience complete joy and ecstasy after this exercise.

The practice of Anter Maun is called mindfulness in the Western world. The effect of this meditation technique can be a life changer because its effect lasts much beyond the time during which Anter Maun is practiced. This creates awareness in a person and leads to control over the mind. In turn, a person takes charge of his life instead of being led by passion and irrational thought processes.

Yoga Nidra

With Anter Maun practice you can become a master of your thoughts and actions. However, an old wise men realized that simply managing your thoughts is not really sufficient to rid yourself completely from misery and sadness. Memories reside in the subconscious and have a tendency to creep up at you when least expected. Unless we go to the root of the problem, which is in the subconscious mind, we will not be able to erase bad thoughts altogether. To achieve this objective you must be able to access your subconscious mind which is only possible through a meditation technique called Yoga Nidra or Yogic sleep.

How to practice Yoga Nidra?

In this type of meditation, you must lie down supine on the ground, with your legs one feet apart and hands next to the body. You already may know that this posture is called Shavasana in Yoga practices. You must close your eyes and take a few deep breaths. Remember that breath is a life force and it energizes the body. In the first phase of Yoga Nidra, you must open your mind to external sounds. You must notice the sounds and rotate your consciousness from one source of sound to another.

In the next phase you must turn your mind inwards. You should concentrate on your breath. Notice the movement of air through your nostrils during inhalation and the exit of warm air during exhalation. Do not force your breath. Your breath should be normal. Follow this process for a couple of minutes. Now shift your focus to your stomach. Your stomach expands and energizes your body when you breathe in. During exhalation your stomach contracts and you feel your body expanding and relaxing. Focusing on your breath will relieve tension from your body. You will feel relaxed. Your mind will feel calm and serene.

At this moment your body is completely relaxed and in near-sleep state and your mind comes in contact with the subconscious. Now you must take a pledge. Your pledge should be simple and must be in accordance with your nature. You may wish whatever you want. Repeat your wish three times with concentration and total commitment. There is a saying that, a wish made in this state of consciousness may come true.

In the third phase of Yoga Nidra, you must now rotate your consciousness through all parts of the body. You must begin with the toes of your right foot. When you see your first toe in your mind, you must say first toe. Likewise you must move up to your hands, fingers, shoulder, back, neck and head. It is said that this practice helps you to reach your inner self or subconscious.

In the fourth phase you must go back to your breath. Notice the inhalation and exhalation of breath through your throat. Feel the warmth of air as it goes out of your throat. Follow this process for a couple of minutes. Now is the time to repeat your vows or pledge. It must be the same as the earlier wish. Repeat three times with total commitment and belief.

In the last phase, you must once again take your mind to the external environment. Slowly become aware of your surroundings – where you are and the sounds around you. You can move your toes and fingers slowly followed by body movements. Now you can open your eyes slowly. Yoga Nidra practice is complete.

The procedure followed in Yoga Nidra is in a way that you are likely to fall asleep. Keep reminding yourself that you are practicing Yoga Nidra. You will derive maximum benefit when you are in a state between wakefulness and sleep. This is the time when your mind can access the subconscious mind. Many strange thoughts and body reactions may be experienced during this state. It is possible that you start weeping or laughing uncontrollably. This happens because your mind experiences sensations which are arising from the subconscious. Many scientists, like Albert Einstein have confessed that their biggest discoveries have happened in a subconscious state. Friedrich August Kekulé is said to have discovered the structure of benzene after dreaming of a snake eating its own tail. Though they may not have called it Yoga Nidra, but the essence of their experience suggests that they may have gone through a mental state which can be achieved through Yoga Nidra. You must remember that Yoga Nidra is only one of the ways to access your subconscious.

If you practice Yoga Nidra on a daily basis, you will be able to access your subconscious. Deep seated thoughts and past fears will emerge from your mind. You need not force yourself to confront the dark past. The cleansing process is automatic and happens without your knowledge. Over a period of time, you will feel relieved of tension.

Practicing Yoga Nidra and Anter Maun together, can bring you to a state of constant bliss and mental peace.

Transcendental meditation

I have discussed the importance of breath earlier. I can go on endlessly about the power of breath and its control. Breath is life force or Prana Shakti. Once you stop breathing you are no more than a dead body. Control of breath is therefore an important aspect of every meditation technique. It is clear that our mind is a monkey. It flits from one thought to another, to the past and into the future. The mind can never be idle. It's like a pot which must contain something. It is filled with air if nothing is poured or kept in it. All meditation techniques are geared towards quietening our mind. Stillness of mind is the ultimate goal. But in today's modern world, we do not have the time or patience to wait to take time to practice until you are able to mindful with just a breathing exercise. In Transcendental meditation, you are required to chant a mantra during the meditation. Chanting of mantra keeps your mind focused.

Maharishi Mahesh Yogi was an Indian philosopher who introduced Transcendental Meditation (TM) to the world. In this technique, you are given a few words to chant while meditating. Every individual has a unique mantra or chant which is provided by a trained practitioner or certified TM teacher. Transcendental meditation can only be learnt by attending a program conducted by certified teachers. However the TM technique is so popular that it is taught even in schools.

There are numerous scientific studies conducted to prove the efficacy of Transcendental meditation. Generally, the accepted belief is that practicing Transcendental meditation leads to a calm and composed mind. It is relaxing and rejuvenating. TM is usually practiced twice daily for a period of ten to twenty minutes, once after breakfast and once before lunch.

Transcendental meditation leads to an altered consciousness, something akin to Yoga Nidra. Therefore practicing Transcendental meditation can be an effective way to access your subconscious. This, in turn, can change your perspective towards life. Many psychological problems like depression can be managed effectively by using Transcendental meditation along with medication.

There are contrarian views regarding the Transcendental meditation technique. Some reports suggest that the effect of TM is as good as keeping your eyes closed. Such a view ignores the fact that TM is not only about keeping your eyes closed. It's much more than that. Ultimately, it's the massive popularity of Transcendental meditation which proves the point.

Guided Meditation

This is an easy meditation practice especially for those who find it difficult to concentrate on their own. Guided meditation relaxes the body and calms the mind. There are many variations to guided meditation.

The one I prefer is a soothing voice taking you through various stages of this meditation. The guidance is accompanied by soothing background instrumental music. Sometimes the sounds of nature, like birds chirping in the morning, itself acts as meditation. I often spend a few minutes listening to sounds of nature especially early in the morning. It elevates the soul and brings immense calmness in my mind. It prepares me for the day's work.

I have discovered that the main ingredient of guided meditation is an isolated place which is free of distractions like the noise of traffic or the TV blaring away from a neighbor's window. Such interference makes me irritated and takes me away from my intended goal. Initially, I could concentrate only when there were no distractions. Gradually I have now developed the ability to concentrate even when there is noise. I would advise beginners to find a place which is free of noise initially.

In the practice of guided meditation you can use either visual or audio clues. Some people naturally respond favorably to visuals while others may be stimulated by audio. A combination of visual and aural stimulation is also possible. The goal, as such, is to relax your mind. On the other hand, you may feel that visuals may actually detract from concentrating on the meditation practice.

What is the goal of a guided meditation? In this meditation technique you use the body as a medium to achieve calmness. In the beginning, you must choose a point on your body which will help you to relax. For example, I find the stomach a good place to begin. You must watch the stomach expand and contract with the intake and exhalation of breath. When you take in the breath, your body expands and energizes. Feel the energy flowing through your body, filling you with vitality. Hold the breath for a few seconds. Slowly exhale and let the air out of your body. Let the body relax. Feel the tension ebbing from your body. Let go. Don't hold back.

In the second phase, follow the guided meditation. At this stage, your mind and body are completely relaxed, ready to accept the guidance without holding back. I hope to talk about guided meditation in a separate book, but for now I will encourage readers to explore this kind of meditation on their own.

Body scan meditation

Body scan meditation is another easy practice. I have covered this process earlier, in combination with mindfulness techniques. I am mentioning it separately here, because you can benefit greatly by performing Body scan meditation as a standalone practice.

It is surprising when you think that very few of us are actually aware of our own bodies. We take our body for granted – after all you were born with it. However, becoming aware of different parts of our body can be a revelation of sorts. In Body scan meditation, you must lie down, either on a hard bed or on the floor. Ensure that your body does not slump.

Begin this practice by concentrating on your right foot. Feel the toes, the sole, the heel and the foot as a whole. Contemplate on the right foot. Fill your thoughts with the image of your foot. Let go of all other thoughts.

Move from the right foot to the left foot. Gradually, include both your legs. Concentrate. What do you feel? Can you feel the muscles of your thigh and the buttocks? Do not make any movement. Feel the muscles of your legs and relax. Remember that you are not to move your body parts. Move toward your stomach an upward slowly. Go up till your head. Feel your forehead relax and the facial muscles go slack. The entire process should take around ten minutes.

Your focus must begin from a small portion of the body like your toe and encompass the entire boy. Move your focus from minute details to a wider awareness of your body.

Body scan meditation prepares you for the practice of mindfulness. You can make it a part of your regular routine. It is a good alternative to Yoga Nidra and Anter Maun, though not as powerful. On some days, you may not have the time to go through the entire gamut of mindfulness practice. On those days you can do a quick ten minute body scan to become relaxed.

Metta or loving kindness

Don't think that Metta or loving kindness is the least important practice because I have discussed it last. Ironically, I have found it to be the most difficult and also the easiest meditation practice. Difficult because loving others unequivocally and without rancor and resentment is tough. It is easy because it is our natural state but has been hidden from our awareness due to our ignorance.

I find Metta as the most beautiful and elevating meditation practice. I was captivated by the simplicity of this technique. It takes you through various stages of loving kindness.

Like many other meditation practices, you can begin the practice of Metta or loving kindness by sitting in a comfortable lotus position with feet folded under the legs and hands resting gently on your knees. You can take the support of the wall or any solid object to keep your spine erect. If you are unable to assume the lotus position, you can sit in any position; only remember to keep your back straight.

Begin by concentrating on your breath. As I have already mentioned, breath is the bridge between the mind and body. Feel the cool air enter your nostrils and warm air leave.

Slowly feel the air encompass your entire self. Feel yourself surrounded by warmth. Feel the glow around you. You are inside a cocoon of kindness and compassion. At this juncture you may hold your arms around your body in a gentle hug. Look at your body through the mind's eye. Feel the love and deep adoration. Slowly, chant in your mind- May I be happy, May I be healthy. May I be serene, May I be peaceful. Repeat every thirty seconds while in the embrace of warmth. Let the words sink into your very being.

The first part of Metta or loving kindness is focused on oneself. The basic concept of this Metta philosophy is that you cannot love others unless you love yourself first. It is essential that you let the feeling of loving kindness permeate into you. At this stage remain focused on your own self. Let the love, affection and adoration slowly engulf you. This is an easy exercise because by nature we love ourselves.

After a few minutes, bring a person who is close to your heart, into the sphere of warmth, love and affection which you have embraced. A mother can think of her children, a lover can think of the partner, a child can think of the mother; anyone who you have genuine feelings for. Do not feign love. Do not try to include someone out of pity. There has to be genuine affection.

Now repeat in your mind - May you be happy, May you be healthy, May you be serene, May you be peaceful.

Pass your loving kindness to the person who is now in your sphere of warmth. Connect the feelings arising in your mind an let them flow easily towards the other person.

In the third phase, bring in others into your sphere loving influence. Expand your embrace. Let others also be engulfed in your feeling of Metta or loving kindness. I will suggest that you develop your own phrases which represent your feelings better. This will make it easier to practice Metta or loving kindness.

During this practice you may experience the unexpected. Sometimes instead of loving kindness you may feel sad. You may get angry and hurt. Do not blame yourself when this happens. Do not take it as your failure. This is a sign that your heart is softening. Use patience to resolve the contradictions. You can slowly break from Metta and resume after some time.

Conclusion

What did you learn from this book? Meditation is not one technique or method or process. Meditation is not simply a mental exercise. It has a goal and that is to attain happiness and joy in life. For most people it is a practical method of improving everyday performance and controlling stress in daily life.

I have dwelt in detail on various meditation techniques which enhance the experience of mindfulness. Use them as the medium or support to eventually master mindfulness.

There are a number of key elements which, if properly attended to, will greatly enhance your experience of mindfulness. At this stage, I am no longer bothered with those who are well on their way to achieving mindfulness. This book has enough material to guide them through the process. I want to once again go through some vital steps required to be taken by a beginner. To the uninitiated beginner, the steps listed below may seem mundane and unimportant on a first reading. Experience however has shown that they exert a subtle (but important) influence.

Step #1: Designating a quiet secluded place for meditation.

Step #2: Choosing a proper time (which is one's 'right' time) for meditation. This could be early in the morning before starting the day's activities. The peace from meditating will radiate throughout the day. The other chosen time could be just before going to bed at night. This will enhance the soundness of sleep.

Step #3: Sitting straight and relaxed while meditating. The best is to sit on the floor on a cushion. If this is not possible, a low stool or even a chair will do fine. The important thing is to assume an erect but relaxed sitting posture. There is no need to assume a yogic posture.

Step #4: Preparing physically like taking a shower (or at least washing face and hands), wearing loose-fitting clothes, taking off one's shoes etc. improves the quality of meditation.

Step #5: Closing one's eyes for meditating is important for beginners. There are proponents of 'open-eyed' meditation, with a candle or a flower as the object of concentration. The sensory perceptions when eyes are open are too powerful for beginners to overcome. In such a situation, the meditation is ineffective.

Step #6: Increasing the duration of mindfulness incrementally is the key to success. In the beginning just 5 minutes of mindfulness, once in the morning and again at night, is generally enough. More than 5 minutes at a time may increase mental tension and be counter-productive. The duration can be gradually increased over a period to 10 minute sessions.

If these simple steps (not necessarily in the order they are written) are followed, mindfulness will help one to achieve deep levels of mental rest and become a much more calm, happy and relaxed person.

I hope the readers would have taken this opportunity to expand their vision and experience the beauty of mindfulness. I have benefitted greatly from these very techniques and I am sure everyone can.

May you be mindful all the time! May your life be filled with happiness, joy and bliss!

References

i. https://en.oxforddictionaries.com/definition/mind

ii. https://kadampa.org/reference/mind

iii. https://kadampa.org/books/understanding-the-mind

iv. https://www.nhs.uk/Tools/Pages/Mood-self-assessment.aspx?Tag=Mental+health

v. https://www.nhs.uk/Tools/Pages/Mood-self-assessment.aspx?Tag=Mental+health

vi. https://www.bemindfulonline.com/test-your-stress/

vii. http://www.stress.org.uk/individual-stress-test/

&c.

42612539R00031

Made in the USA
Middletown, DE
16 April 2019